Life Must Be Heard

Life Must Be Heard

Marilyn D. Priester

authorHOUSE®

AuthorHouse™
1663 Liberty Drive
Bloomington, IN 47403
www.authorhouse.com
Phone: 1-800-839-8640

Published by AuthorHouse   02/15/2012

ISBN: 978-1-4685-5323-9 (sc)
ISBN: 978-1-4685-5304-8 (ebk)

Library of Congress Control Number: 2012903046

Any people depicted in stock imagery provided by Thinkstock are models, and such images are being used for illustrative purposes only.
Certain stock imagery © Thinkstock.

This book is printed on acid-free paper.

Because of the dynamic nature of the Internet, any web addresses or links contained in this book may have changed since publication and may no longer be valid. The views expressed in this work are solely those of the author and do not necessarily reflect the views of the publisher, and the publisher hereby disclaims any responsibility for them.

FOR RAY MY HUSBAND AND MY
WONDERFUL BROTHER WILLIAM DAVIS JR
24 MAY 1968 – 14 JULY 2007

ACKNOWLEDGMENTS

First I would like to thank God who is the head of my life. I'm very grateful to have been able to actually express what's on my heart. To include have a very strong husband that supported me through a lot and encourage me to do this. I can not forget all the love and support my family gave me as well.

My poetry is dedicated to my family and friends. I've been writing poetry all my life but, only allowing my family and close friends to read what I've been writing. Now God has given me the strength to let the world read it as well.

I'll leave you with some encouraging words; always remember, surround yourself with positive people saying and doing positive things while never deviating from your plans.

Thank You,
Marilyn D. Priester

CONTENTS

Chapter One (A Little Help From Above) 1

God's Gift 2
Going Through 3
Thanksgiving 4
One Day 5
Not Finished 6
Pray With Me 7
Life 8
God Said 9
The Light 11
Angels 12
Soul Searching 13
Silver And Gold 14
A Christmas Prayer 15
Why I Sing 16
The Price 18
You Gave 19
Crying Out 20

Chapter Two (Family Life) 21

Brothers 22
Cooking 23
A Daughter's Love 24
Private Dancer 25
The Man 26
The Under Dog 27
My Grandmother 28
Hard Times 29
A Mother's Love 30
Movin Up 32
Husband Of Mine 34
Phases Of Love 35
Compliment 36
Military 37
A Soldier's Request 38
You Hurt Me 39
A Father's Blessing 40
A Friend Of Mine 41

Changes 42

Myself 43

Times Have Changed 44

I Wanna 45

Chicken Noodle Soup 46

You Are What You Are 47

Mess'n Around 48

The Presents Of A Woman 49

Class Reunion 50

Military Wife 51

 Understanding Me 52

Work It Out 54

Leaving The Nest 55

Lie-Ba-Tion 56

Center Of Attraction 57

Piece Of Mind 58

Talk To Me 59

Paranoid 60

Got Played 62

Made It 63

Life Lessons 64

A New Beginning 66

Jennie In The Bottle 67

Deception 68

Timeless 69

In-Fake-Tu-Ation 70

Hounding Me 71

Too Young 72

Chapter Three (History for You) 73

Take My Picture (Part One) 74

Chains 75

Buffalo Soldier 77

Freedom Train 78

Chapter Four (Street Life) 79

Pusher Man 80

Black Warrior 81

The Stroll 82

Fast Lane 83

The Loot 85

Grind 'N 86

Corner Hustle 87

Face Off 88

Chapter Five (Thoughts of You) 89

    September Rain... 90

    Sex As A Weapon 91

    Winter Blues.. 92

    Missing You 93

    Daddy's Little Girl 94

    Just Me 95

    Diva.. 96

    My Little Brother.. 98

    Dreams 99

    You're Holding Back 100

    Love.. 101

    You And Me.. 102

    Emotions 103

    Pledge My Love 104

Chapter One

A Little Help From Above

GOD'S GIFT

Have you ever had something so precious in life; I prayed and asked GOD to put a special woman into my life; someone that will be my faithful companion so, he blessed me with my wife

They say the man is the head of the house; but it wouldn't be no head without my wife, she keeps me strong and encourage me to keep building our foundation instead

It's my wife that makes our house a place where we can call home; every day I thank GOD for blessing me with such a strong courageous woman

She's always there for me; lifting me up and bringing out the best in me

She always know when something is wrong; then she would smile, and say baby we'll work it out, we always do and true enough GOD heard her too

I can never stop expressing my love for my wife, because it was GOD that brought her right into my life

I'll ask you again; have you ever had something so precious that you would give your life? I do and it's my loving wife

GOING THROUGH

GOD says daily, hold on and don't bend in the road 'cause the devil is waiting
to take your soul

Follow your dreams and never let anyone take your things; no matter what life
throws your way, stay stead fast and it'll all pass

Remember stay out of the past; move forward and make things last, 'cause the future
is where it's at, as a matter of fact you know GOD always had your back

Everyday there's someone try n to take your blessed spirit away; please don't let the
devil have it all his way

You keep doing what you do just pray, pray, pray and blessings will soon come your way;
then you thank GOD for listening to you that day

You know life has its setbacks just always stay positive; and take one day at a time, only
GOD need to know what you're going through

Stay focused and stick to your plan; 'cause in the end GOD made sure your feet stayed
planted firmly in his hands

THANKSGIVING

Being alive to see another day

Look at how you have changed

Watching your family grow

Giving guidance to who need it the most

Not realizing that everyday there's something to be thankful for

So; look around the dinner table and just say, we will all pray on this
Thanksgiving Day

ONE DAY

We'll make it for sure one day; all we have to do is bow our heads and pray

Never forget who helped us get that way; or GOD will surly take it all away

We've given so much to people each and every day; because we know GOD has made us humble that way

We have to hold on; 'cause GOD knows that it want be long for us to make it one day

Our day will come when we least expect it; so let's not change we'll just thank GOD and respect it one day

NOT FINISHED

I look over my life several times and wonder just how I came this far; I know GOD is not finished with me yet

Each and every day becomes a challenge that only he knows just how much I can bear; I know GOD is not finished with me yet

Taking one day at a time seems like forever but, when I'm dispirited I just look into the sky and say; I know GOD is not finished with me yet

Sometimes I can almost feel the devil right upon my heels wanting me to do something wrong; when he knows I'm trying to change my life, then I say to the devil I know you're a liar; 'cause GOD is not finished with me yet

The more I pray the more I see my life changing for the better and he's enriching my life to the fullest; why I know this because GOD is not finished with me yet

Just as he is blessing me continuously he can do the same for you just believe that; GOD is not finished with you yet

PRAY WITH ME

Why do you need to know who am I? Just pray with me

I once lived, had to carry my own cross, then was crucified; not knowing
why all this was bestowed upon me

Darkness covered the sky, then the light shined through, I was born again and
all your sins were lifted too

I'm now called GOD of all GODS, king of all kings; you shall not put no one before
me; because you just don't know how priceless I can be, until you take the time to pray
with me

You say, how can all this be? Stay humble and listen then you'll see how blessed your
family life can be

Remember I'm more than beauty itself; so don't envy anyone else, when your feelings
are low, get on your knees and pray with me; and tell the devil this is not his show

No matter what; I'll never let you go, all I ask is sometimes just pray with me and you'll
always have that glow 'cause I'm JESUS CHRIST, so now you know

LIFE

Life is like a moving locomotive within a blink of an eye it will pass you by

Stop worrying about the small things; take time out to enjoy the happiness
that life brings

Why be stressed with a whole lot of mess; just thank GOD and be blessed

Life had its ups and downs but, that doesn't mean you have to wear a frown

Take time out and enjoy your life at its best and forget about the rest

GOD SAID

GOD said, why are you worried put all your burdens on me

I already know just how much you can bear

Little do you know, I already picked you up and turned you around

Right now your feet is already placed on higher ground

Keep putting your faith in me and read your bible more than watching TV

I've already blessed you more than you'll ever know

Open your eyes and your heart; then you'll see your blessings grow

I may not come when you want me to but; I always come on time so leave all
your worries behind

THE LIGHT

I'm looking into this wonderful light, Lord are you calling on me; is it my time to go?
I haven't seen my grandchildren grow

So why, oh why must I go; I thought the reaper would deceive me but, he lead me
straight to thee, Lord just as I served you on earth

I'll do the same upon my rebirth; I'll give signs to my children below, letting them know
there will always be an angel watching you grow

ANGELS

Angels are sent from heaven to give blessings and brighten someone's day

When you see babies smiling in their sleep those are angels tickling their little feet

The lord send angels each and every day; sometimes angels are born then taken away

Angels are like rainbows in the sky their always happy while leading you to that special place

When an angel comes and tell you it's time don't resist just grab their hands; because GOD said you have to go

SOUL SEARCHING

Some days my heart and soul is filled with loneliness; it's like going through a tunnel of darkness
waiting to see the light on the other side

Happiness is what I'm searching for; my soul has traveled deep into the heart of others only to find
out they are not what I seek

Looking deep into a person's soul can tell you a lot; it'll let you know if their willing to give their
heart

I've searched high and low to find that happiness glow; but nonetheless no one showed

Soul searching is very hard to do; when happiness suppose to be shared by two

Now I'm wondering just what to do; when GOD spoke to me and said happiness was already
inside you

SILVER AND GOLD

I thought it was nothing more wonderful than the thirst for silver and gold

While searching for those precious things in life; I found out that my search was really to find
Christ

Silver and gold are the most valuable medals you can hold; but, understand this their nothing
without Christ in your soul

So my quest was never to find silver and gold; but to have Christ in my life; now that's a story to be
told 'cause it's worth more than silver and gold

A CHRISTMAS PRAYER

Listen; there's a strong silence through this old house

All are rested and put to sleep; it's a time where everyone should be at peace

Say a little Christmas prayer 'cause Gods angels will bare witness there

No matter what you're going through GOD will show you the light

Did you know it was that star shining on Christmas night?

The three kings brought gifts because it was a wonderful sight

A child was born to bring joy to the world

So, don't forget to say a little Christmas prayer on this warm winter night

'Cause the child's name was Jesus Christ

WHY I SING

I sing when I praise the lord 'cause it lifts me up high

I sing because my children are always asking why

I sing when thinking of my brother while trying not to cry

I sing because the birds fly high in the sky

I sing and thank GOD for giving me such a blessed day

Finally, I sing because I'm happy and no one can take that away

This is why I sing

THE PRICE

The price we pay is not much; when JESUS gave his life to save us

The price we pay for not receiving that blessing coming our way

We're always asking for this and asking for that; don't you know GOD got our backs

He'll give us what we need; all he ask is to pray and learn to take heed

The price we pay waiting on Jesus Christ to return

The price we pay just to live at least one more day; not knowing when GOD will take us all away

The price we pay is not much; so, thank GOD just for waking you up 'cause the price we pay really is not that much

YOU GAVE

Lord you gave me the wisdom to think wisely

You gave me the knowledge to know all the days would be long

You gave me the faith to always hold on

You gave me a heart to love all others

You gave me joy to praise you the almighty above

But, most of all you gave me life

CRYING OUT

I see your pain all over your face; you're crying out but, yet no one can hear you in this place

Your pain is more than anyone else can bear; how can you keep crying out when only GOD truly care

Release your fears and just let go with warm flowing tears; 'because your cry is silent even the angels can't hear

This is the point in your life that you need to cry out; but don't know how cause you thought GOD had tuned you out

So, cry out loud as you can; then get on your knees and ask GOD for his helping hand

Because it was GOD that had you crying out; letting you know he never once left your side and was there when you needed him the most

Now, there's nothing wrong with crying out; that is God's way of getting you to listen; by saying my child please pay attention

Chapter Two

Family Life

BROTHERS

They are bonded for life just like husband and wife; they pledge to be my brother's keeper while their bond grows deeper

You'll never have to fear because they'll always be near

My brother's are very unique they help others reach their peak; they are on so many levels while still respecting the other fellow

People say they have lots of secrets but, how can that be when they go way down into history

No matter what they say there's always a brother with that attentive ear bearing witness to what he hear; just keep in mind one of those brothers just might be mine

COOKING

My man cooks for me; how wonderful that can be

Take a seat baby and rest your feet; I want you to relax and eat

I'm your chef today; and you don't even have to pay

I can see how wonderful it can be when my husband cooks for me

A DAUGHTER'S LOVE

Momma you made a choice to bring me into this world your beautiful black girl; you
worked several jobs to make ends meet, so I would have food to eat

You always said, a black woman have to stay strong in order to get ahead; you told me
keep my head held high and reach for the sky

You would always say, never forget your dreams and don't let obstacles get in between; when
I didn't have no answer at all you gave me advice and said pray on it not once but twice

Momma you always told me that the road wouldn't be easy; when I would feel down you
would say, girl pick-up your face and get back in the race

And don't worry about what people have to say; you're a strong black woman and GOD can see;
momma I know you'll always be proud of me because I'm the image truly from thee

PRIVATE DANCER

Soon as you walked into the room, their eyes were glued right on you; they all
are waiting to see who will get the first dance

Now all eyes are on you and your first victim too; so go ahead don't be ashamed
you are a private dancer

A dancer for money 'cause that's what you do

Every night the place is packed 'cause everyone heard how good you are; so they all
want to dance only with you

You teach these men and some ladies too, how to dance the night away without anyone
step'n all on your shoe

You teach them to move with lots of grace even though sometimes they quickly loose
their pace

While encouraging them to keep up the good work; a great big smile comes upon their
face

Which lets you know in your heart; that's why you became a private dancer in the first
place

THE MAN

This man has been in my life since I've been born; this man has taught me many
many things how to be respected and respect others

And being the head of the house is what a real man is about; always sure our family
is never without

This man has taught me to stand proud and never back down but, do know what battles
to fight and the one's to let go

This man has been my mentor for life; time after time he has given me advice, he said
always put GOD ahead of your life and take your time choosing your wife

This man has never steered me wrong he said, son now is the time for you to make a life
of your own

Build a foundation and keep it strong; this man standing tall and bold is my father; he has
taught me many things so, now that I'm grown I can teach my own

THE UNDER DOG

You must don't know how messy people can be

If only they could accept me just being me

I try to do my best and stay out of mess

Every day I go to work and say; GOD please don't let me be stressed

I know people are actually doing me wrong

Because then they start singing that old song

But, nonetheless I continue to put a smile on my face

'Cause little do they know I'm working hard to get out of this gossipin place

MY GRANDMOTHER

My grandmother is special as she can be; she has created a beautiful family tree

My grandmother sits on the porch in her rocking chair; while I grease her scalp and
Comb her hair

Grandma said, child look at all this land; it will be here for every generation to see
I worked this land all my life; then right before Mr. Johnson died he sold it all to me

Eighty acres and a house by an old oak tree

Grandma said, I was born on this land and my momma before me, then I had your momma
So, that's how you came to be

Then grandma said, you see child how this land goes way back into the family tree?

So, once you get old as me you can tell your grandchildren about how they came to be;
While sittin under the old oak tree

HARD TIMES

I'm catching hard times; my bills are late, there's no food on my plate

My kids just whine, whine, whine 'cause I don't have a dime

Oh Lord, why am I catching such a hard time?

I've been looking for jobs here and there but, no one is hiring anywhere
I'm trying to get on my feet

So, I can make ends meet; bottom line hard times just got me beat

A MOTHER'S LOVE

I made a choice to bring you into this world my beautiful black girl; I worked several jobs to make ends meet so I could have food for you to eat

I always told you to stay strong in order to get ahead; I told you to keep your head held high and reach for the sky

I would always say, never forget your dreams and don't let obstacles get in between; when you didn't have no answer at all I gave you advice and said; pray on it not once but twice

I always told you that the road wouldn't be easy; when you would feel down I would tell you girl pick-up your face and get back in the race

And don't worry about what people say, you're a strong black woman and GOD can see; I will always be proud of you, because you are the image truly from thee

MOVIN UP

We're finally movin up; we had a long road ahead

But, with hard work and a little prayer we made it instead

Never forget where you came from

Just as fast as you received it; oh yes GOD will retrieve it

Always remember, GOD will show you the way so grab hold to others to
make their day

HUSBAND OF MINE

My husband is wonderful indeed

He keeps me pleased with all the lovin' I need

He buys me beautiful things to include the bling, bling

He keeps me close to his heart even when we're apart

He's my knight in shiny armor ensuring no harm comes to me

My husband is the best; which puts him beyond the rest

PHASES OF LOVE

Phase one; make love to me soft and tenderly by touching my body very
gracefully making every touch more special than the last

Phase two; make love to me with your beautiful brown eyes which makes
me feel so warm inside

Phase three; make love to me by touching my heart with those special words
you say to me

Phase four; I'm on top of the world when you make love to me so passionately

COMPLIMENT

Girl, you sho lookin good with yo smooth brown skin, hair done just right

A body shaped like one of those old coke cola bottles; yo nickname must be cola,
'cause you sho nuff 28 in the waist and fine in the face

Girl with a body like that you make a brother wanna give you all his check; I can tell
You from the old school so, I'm not tryin to play you like a fool

Or run any game 'cause mackaville is not my name; I'll leave you with this, you are one
Beautiful black sis

MILITARY

I've been to several countries throughout my life

I've seen things that were only in your dreams

I've been in two major wars fighting for my countries way of life

Leaving my family not only once but twice

I've received several distinguished medals by helping out my countries
fallen fellows

While you go about your day; remember it's a soldier that has paved the way

A SOLDIER'S REQUEST

Dress me up in my Army greens; put a smile on my face 'cause I'm going to
my final resting place

Have me displayed so all can see how an Army soldier should be

Then close my casket and cover me with the greatest flag of all

After I receive my burial honors present this flag to the one that bears
no tears and standing tall

It was a great honor to serve my country; so keep this flag in remembrance
of me throughout all eternity

YOU HURT ME

You hurt me with your words

'Cause you're listening to things you heard

You hurt me bringing up the past

Hey, I'm busting my butt to make this last

You hurt me when you don't trust me

'Cause you're too busy trying to bust me

You hurt me when you shout

It makes me want to get out

You hurt me when you keep reminding me of what I use to be

That's no longer it; so can you please stop hurting me before I have a fit

A FATHER'S BLESSING

You've given so much encouragement to whom need it the most; and lots
of advice not once but more than twice

You worked hard to see your family grow; while each and every day you pray,
lord I thank you for this blessed day

You're one of a kind and you just happen to be mine

Your son will be truly an image of thee a father's blessing coming from within
me

Your daughter, even though she looks like me, on her wedding day she too will have
her father's blessing that all can see

No matter what, through thick or thin you'll always be a father's blessing to me

GOD has given me a blessing, my husband a wonderful man indeed; that take care
of all his family needs

A FRIEND OF MINE

You are a friend of mine; we'll stay in touch throughout time

You are a friend of mine; you were there when I was going through a bad situation

You are a friend of mine; you listen when I felt like talking

You are a friend of mine; you allowed me to be myself, expressing my feelings the
only way I know how

You are a friend of mine; even though we don't talk every day I thank GOD for you anyway

You are a friend of mine; every day I pray, Lord let my friend have a blessed day

'Cause you are a friend of mine; people come and people go but, one thing for sure
friends will always show

You are a friend of mine; we must stay in touch, 'cause that's how friends love each other
so much

I'll treasure your friendship forever and will come to help you in any type of weather

You are a friend of mine

CHANGES

One day you were on top of the world; being showered with diamonds and pearls

Over the past years he almost destroyed you mentally and tried to do it physically

You're put last when you should actually be treated first class

You don't express your feelings much because you know he'll get bucked

You finally opened your eyes to see he cannot let go of his kid's momma; tell'n you
he's just try'n to keep down drama

He use to write you lots of notes and on occasion maybe tell you a joke

You asked yourself what happened to the man that swept you off your feet

Your heart is broken into two parts; one wants to stay the other say leave and get
a new start

Tell'n you he loves you made your day; but now he don't even look your way

Stop try'n and try'n 'cause all it's doing is keeping you cry'n and cry'n

It takes two to make a relationship work; so if you see he's not going to meet you half
way

Move on with your life 'cause he really didn't want you as his wife

MYSELF

I was so busy expressing my love in so many ways; I completely forgot
to start loving myself

A lot of things I say; and a lot I don't say, only because I've learned to
be humble that way

I speak my mind to let you know; I'm a woman that will never let her
independence go

I've fallen down many of times; but only to get back up, because my mother
raised me to never give up and stay in the fight 'til I finally get it right

I've learned not to worry about what people say; and to accept all my imperfections
because GOD made me that way

I've learned never to take life for granted; 'cause we all are seeds that GOD had planted

As I look back on my life; I wouldn't change a thing, because those bumps in the road is
what made me the strong woman I am today

While GOD keeps giving blessings my way; I've learned to give him praise each and every day,
I've learned with GODS helping hands, now I can finally start to love me, by being myself

TIMES HAVE CHANGED

Times have changed on how the military use to be

There once was a time when discipline was the key

Making you proud to wear the uniform; and fight for your countries
freedom either on land or at sea

There once was a time when leadership meant a lot to you and me

Back in the day you were trained as a Soldier first and fighting as a team

While teaching you pride and lots of self esteem

The chain of command back in the day actually lead the way

But, with what's going on today; all their worried about is how much pay

You know back in the day rank was earned now it's just given away

Times have changed as you can see; keep watching your TV

That'll tell you just how the military is going to be

I WANNA

Sometimes, it takes only a start to make your dreams come true

You let situations decide on what you really wanna do

You already know how to make it happen; 'cause it's been going through
your mind like a fox chasing a rabbit

Stop listening to those fools that don't have a clue and listen to your heart
it'll tell you what to do

While you start to do your own thing; remember grinning is what you must do
in order to get people to see just what you do

So let your talents shine through; now once you realize to focus

Then finally all your dreams will come true

CHICKEN NOODLE SOUP

Chicken noodle soup is real good from what I've been told

To include chicken noodle soup is good for your soul; so why don't you
take a seat and taste a bowl

You can bet this chicken noodle soup is the best; 'cause it's made from
scratch

It taste so good it'll have you purring like a kitty cat; chicken noodle soup does
more than just calm you down

It'll put your body at ease; while telling your mind to eat some more please

Eating chicken noodle soup will never get old; 'cause just having one bowl it brings
out a great conversation

Then allows you tell things that have never been told; I guess chicken noodle soup
is worth its weight in gold

So, the next time you wanna talk to get things off yo chest and to put yo mind to rest;
jus come on by, then step into my kitchen to have yourself a little bowl

YOU ARE WHAT YOU ARE

Look into the mirror and see that beautiful face; while your head is held high with lots of grace
Look into the mirror and see that beautiful body; with an even skin tone from head to toe, don't be afraid to let your imperfections show
Look into the mirror and see that you have people guessing your age; with no wrinkles truly they should know this is not staged
Your beauty comes from your family tree; with only your ancestors knowing the secrets that all can see
Look into the mirror and see that you are one of a kind and everything about you is as it should be
Look into the mirror and say, I realize that only GOD is better than me

MESS'N AROUND

Who you wanna be? You silly clown you're try'n to make a name for yourself
by mess'n around all over town

My friends and family warned me of this; now every time I think of it I just get pissed

You're not the man I thought you would be; instead all along you've been just tell'n lies
to me

We always fuss and fight; then later you want to make up think'n everything alright

Face it you're too stuck on yourself to even care 'bout anyone else

What happen to I'll shower you with lots of diamonds and pearls; all you been doing is
running around with lots of girls

You've put me through too much mess and keeping me stressed

I can't tolerate this anymore; right now you need to pack your things and head out that door

THE PRESENTS OF A WOMAN

GOD saw that Adam was lonely; he put him to sleep and created this woman

Her presents is so strong, throughout each century she has made men weak

When she walks into a room, men quickly stand to their feet

She fall under so many categories; a daughter, sister, and some day in her life
to be someone's wife

This woman has made a wonderful sacrifice by giving me life; and her heart is so big,
she even adopted some play kids

The lord has blessed this woman in so many ways, I'll make sure she don't have to
work in her old days

The presents of this woman will always keep me strong; this WOMAN is my mother

GOD has given her all the glory to be able to tell her story on this magnificent mother's day

CLASS REUNION

Some work'n hard to get ahead; some just sleep all day in bed

Some still look the same; while some look bad 'cause their on that thang

Some dealing drugs and at the same time watch'n their grave being dug

Some moved away 'cause they had enough of this place

Some are living in jail without any bail

Some have turned out to be motivational speakers

While some are just driving around adjusting their loud tweeters

Some have turned out to be complete drunks; while sit'n on their hang out stomp

Some are sit'n around hope'n on a whole lot of maybes; while make'n lots of babies

Some were just killed 'cause of being in the wrong places; jus so happen all these people
are my class mates

MILITARY WIFE

My life was full of surprises; once I became a military wife

I was a stay at home mom; when my husband said I must go and detect some
bombs

I instantly became the dad; while trying to raise a teenage son

Getting a job to help ends meet was too easy; when just the other day
I was folding sheets

Being a military wife is not easy as you may think; because watching the news
everyday kept me on my feet

Praying that they don't call out my husband's last name

I wouldn't trade my marriage for nothing in the world; 'cause I'm waiting on my husband
to finally come home to see his baby girl

Like I said as a military wife my life was full of surprises; and I thank GOD for allowing
my husband to see many sun rises

UNDERSTANDING ME

You always knew when I was not in a good mood but yet; you still allowed
me to be myself

You've always been so understanding; just how a husband should be

Even when my attitude was a little nasty; you never forgot a birthday, anniversary
or that just because gift, only you know how to make my emotions shift

Sometimes I would take your patients to a new level; but nonetheless you still remained
that smooth talking fellow

You made sure my stress level stayed down no matter how much I might clown; it's
so amazing just how much you understand me

You make others sick with envy; while being that faithful husband only giving your love
to your wife, and using my heart just to keep understanding how happy you've made me

You protect your home like you should do; but never taking my independence away from me;
that's because you really understand how a woman should be

You have a gift no other man has; being my wonderful husband who always understood me

WORK IT OUT

There's no doubt what it's all about

Stop pouting and shouting before they all find out

You love me and I love you; now you should know I can't live
without my boo

You're in or out please let's find out what the problem is all about

Love me or leave me; so please stop teasing me

Look you're all about me; I'm all about you; so let's stop playing and do
what we're gonna do

'Cause I just can't live without my boo

LEAVING THE NEST

Little baby bird you must try to fly; so you can leave this nest

Oh, baby bird you must do your best; I have to put your flying skills to the test

If you fall to the ground; get back up and try to fly around

You have the whole world ahead of you; so try to see your life through

Baby bird you'll never forget where your nest is at; 'cause no matter what you
can always come back and take a rest

Don't be afraid of what your life will bring; just accept it and shake yourself clean

My little baby bird

LIE-BA-TION

I love feeling good when I wake up in the morning and all through the day

On weekends we sit and talk 'bout the good old times; while I'm sip'n on that moon shine

I can turn it on and turn it off; I jus don't want people think'n I'm soft

When I'm on that oil I wanna get busy in the sheets; but my shorty say can you please jus go to sleep

People say when I get drunk up; well I'm the life of the party, I don't know 'cause I jus can't remember it

My family keep telling me I'm not myself; 'cause that LIE-ba-tion got me addicted like a junky look'n for their next fix

I keep saying I'm gone quit, but that LIE-ba-tion jus keep calling me back to take another hit

Let the truth be told; this is a life experience that you can win; 'cause that LIE-ba-tion was never your friend

CENTER OF ATTRACTION

Everything must go my way; hold up that's not what I want even though it's not my day

I wanna change my outfit too 'cause I can't have the honoree try'n to out dress me

I'm sit'n at the head table with my family on display; I must make my move before they take the cameras off me too soon

I made a speech just all 'bout me; even though I was not the honoree; being the center of attraction is what I must be

I gave you a moment to say what was on your mind; so please note I have to be the center of attraction just one last time

I never knew that being the center of attraction meant so much to me; when actually you should have been the celebrity

PIECE OF MIND

Sometimes I just wanna piece of mind

Whining down is what I like to do after working hard all day

So quiet time is what I need to keep my mind at ease

Yes, I do love that alone time and to sip on some red wine

Always relax and remember the thought of the day

Then close your eyes and let your mind just take you away

Having a piece of mind at the end of the day; is like going to a silent movie and you don't even
have to pay

TALK TO ME

Why you just don't talk to me; you give advice to everyone but; most importantly not your wife

You put me way back in the line; while on the other hand you talk to your friends at a drop of a dime

When I'm brain storming; sometimes I need to know what you think; not looking at me like my ideas stink

I want my ideas to come to life; support is what I need but, I can't do it without my husband's advice

So, I want ask you twice

PARANOID

Watch what you say; because I just might take it the wrong way

I need to relinquish all those paranoid thoughts; and just ask instead of making myself look like a jackass

It seems like every other year my mind just start kicking into high gear

The things you do and the things you say; got my mind playing tricks on me today

I don't know why I can't trust you; maybe I need to stop holding on to the past; or this relationship just want last

Maybe you're right; this paranoia got me all up tight 'cause what's done in the dark will come to light

'Til then I'll just be cool and everything should be alright

GOT PLAYED

I got played a long time ago; I should've kept that dam wall up

Instead I let my love flow; I didn't see it coming

'Cause dealing with him I let my guard down; now this man got me so dam weak he's making me feel like a circus freak

Getting played was not part of the game; I thought with his admiring words he would still love me just the same

Turned out he was only for himself and not loving anyone else

He started out loving and sharing everything; now I'm just another fling

He played me once; but it'll never happen twice 'cause this time it was the roll of the dice that has made my heart turn cold as ice

MADE IT

Made it is what I've done

Even though people didn't believe in me I still won

I made it with GOD on my side; he told me not to worry; 'cause I'm a blessing in disguise

Now I got people coming from miles around just trying to get down

I quickly had to let them know; back up 'cause you can't get with this flow

When I needed them to understand; they all laughed at me and said; come up with another plan

Since my pockets got fat; I'm laughing now; 'cause I MADE IT! like that

LIFE LESSONS

Throughout your life you are given a lesson; some are good and some are bad

All the life lessons you have had; either you experienced them early or late in life but, you never want to experience them twice

Some life lessons will fill you with pride; while on the other hand life lessons can also make you hide

Life lessons are lessons learned; you can teach people what not to do or how to follow you

Life lessons can be like the river streams; teaching you that there will be obstacles in-between

Remember no life lessons are the same; 'cause on any given day a life lesson will come your way

A NEW BEGINNING

Finally the day has come to see just what history has done

The famous Dr. Martin Luther King "I have a dream" well, it came true for me and you

We can all say there's a black president in office today; even though the struggle was hard and long
but, nonetheless we all stood strong

Keep in mind that racism will never go away with all its many faces; while right now it's just
hiding in little dark places

This day will be marked into the history books; on 4 NOV 2008 the 44th president was a black
man anyway

So, no matter what the out come may bring; still just lift up your voice and sing

JENNIE IN THE BOTTLE

I'll grant your wish but there can only be three 'cause in the end you'll owe me

If this is what you seek; meet me at the crossroad near the dried out creek

Now are you sure; 'cause this is your last chance before we do this dance

Your wishes are granted; so go ahead and live your life

Remember when it's time to pay your debt to me don't think twice

Not realizing that you owed so much; you gave your soul away in just one touch

DECEPTION

People are not who they really seem to be

They are like the reality shows shown on TV

They always ask are you ok; while at the same time talking about you anyway

While their smiling in your face please make sure you kindly put them in their place

When you think you're moving up trust and believe they are trying to find away to mess that up

So, throughout life pay close attention to those you meet

Because it's not by faith their all in your face remember deception is the key

TIMELESS

Timeless is what you are; you have people admiring you from a distance

You show people how to open their hearts and be humble

While letting them know; throughout life we all have taken a little tumble

Your knowledge is beyond approach; but trust me it's your wisdom they seek

Though timeless you may be; when you speak they all listen

"Cause they want to bear witness to what you are preaching

So, timeless is just what you are; 'cause you always teaching

IN-FAKE-TU-ATION

Honey, this man got your mind and gone; he gave you something that you needed to write home

You are in-fake-tu-ated with this man; he has put your body on an all natural high

Don't let this in-fake-tu-ation you are feeling; for this man make you forget why you are trying to change your life

He has told you things you wanted to hear; he even caught you in a time in your life when you are trying to stop being someone else's wife

Please don't get confused cause this man is using all his game tools; he even went on vacation with you just to get even closer

Watch out he's like a wolf in sheep clothing; he will go out of his way to say yes, I had her on the very first day

Hey, you might be thinking; this man is so good to me and that the grass should be greener on the other side

So, once the in-fake-tu-ation is all over the only thing that was greener was your pride

HOUNDING ME

Why you keep trying to push-up on me? It must be something you seek

So don't think for one second you're gonna get me between the sheets

I see your type everyday; full of hype while hoping not to get knocked down in this first round
fight

You keep coming on strong; telling me this and telling me that

But, only for me to say your game ain't tight and as a matter of fact you already lost this first round
fight

So pick-up your pride and walk away at a very quick pace cause the next time I just might have to
slap your face

TOO YOUNG

You are much too young for a real woman like me; you need to focus on what you wanna be

Your body is truly that of an older man; but I'm not the one to teach you 'bout the birds and that honey tree

Just wait, you have time to experience that older woman in life; and yes, she will give you a lesson that will have you thinking twice

Don't try to grow up so fast; but when you do find that first love trust me you're gonna want it to last

Even though you might have kids; well that doesn't constitute for a real man to me

You just got caught between the sheets, 'cause that girl made you weak

One day the light will come on; then you will see, that older woman was just trying to bring out the man in me

Chapter Three

History for You

TAKE MY PICTURE (PART ONE)

Who am I?

Take my picture

Black, bold, strong

Take my picture

African queen or king

Take my picture

No one knows how priceless I can be

Take my picture

I'm more than beauty itself

Take my picture

When I'm gone then you will know

Take my picture

There once lived a blackness that only could show; how everyone wanted
To become a Negro

Take my picture

CHAINS

My ankles are bloody and red from the shackles they shed

My massa got me workin in all this heat; I'm scared to stop

I was told, you keep up the pace or you'll be sold from this place

Massa say, 'round here you work for what you eat; I say Lord jus get me off my feet

I've been wearing these chains for a long time now 'til I'm old and grey

Lord don't make my ancestors pay for what they done to us back in the day

I'm tired and ready to come home; I cannot worry about the family tree, Lord just set me free

BUFFALO SOLDIER

Brown skin color, nappy hair who else can compare

The mighty bison that stands strong and free

You'll represent the 9th and 10th Calvary

Some will forget how you paved the way but, now it's a statue made of you today

Cathay Williams, Mark Matthews to name a few has made history just for you

They served their country well; throughout history you can tell

They were the Buffalo Soldiers that never failed; now we all have a story we can tell

FREEDOM TRAIN

I can't miss that train; I've been running at night and resting during the day

'Cause I know the master got the hunters on the prowl looking for me any way

I'm catching that freedom train yes, I am; I had to leave 'cause the master beat me so, I thought I
was going insane

I left my family behind; they already knew I was pressing for time

Jumping on that freedom train has already made a new man out of me

But, before I left I told my family to pray 'cause your daddy will be back one day

Now since I've became a free man; with my papers in hand; I'll go back and get my family then
buy all masters land

Chapter Four

Street Life

PUSHER MAN

Selling candy is what I do; I'll sell it to your mother, brother, sister and your husband too

I'll make you feel good like you're on top of the world; and don't forget about your girl

I sell candy to the rich and poor whom ever knock on my door; my candy is so good, I'll make you steal from your own hood

Soon you'll start feining for more and more of my special candy

The candy got you turning tricks for all your treats; oh yes! The candy is so, so sweet

You can call me day or night, I'll bring you what you need, so don't beg me please

I sell candy in all shapes and sizes; while putting them in little surprises

Having too much candy can be bad for your health; but it brings me lots of wealth

Some people don't like me; but I be what I be, and no one can take that away from me the Pusher Man

BLACK WARRIOR

You are my black warrior, fighting the poverty that you live in by following the ways of the street life; my black warrior

Doing what had to be done, like making sure the bills got paid, putting food on the table; my black warrior

Praying every night that you finally get it right, before you get put out-of-sight; my black warrior

Now the time has came for you to live right, and be the king of your castle without any hassle; my black warrior

Through thick or thin you'll always win, now that you found peace within; my black warrior

THE STROLL

They were told they have the face and body of a model

They can go far with a body like that; and make lots of cash

Mean while their smoking on all that hash

They start to smile; now they just don't know what to do

While their minds tell them to do what they do

Their completely out of control; while taken that stroll

The stroll got'em in deep; selling their body for lots of drugs

While being beaten down by their thugs

Their so high; not realizing they could die

They once had a face and body like a model

A smile so beautiful it would brighten anyone's place

Now their buried in an unknown space

FAST LANE

Young gifted and black why waste your talent hangin on a corner, so yo boy
can watch your back

You are an entrepreneur through and through; but of the wrong caliber; you rather
sell drugs and steal to pay for your meals

Get your mind out of the gutter; before you catch a case then you'll end up on death
row; watchin the days go by at a very slow pace

'Cause some dude got in yo face; which left you no choice but to take him out, all 'cause
you're not gonna be no bodies girl up in the pen house

Stop before it's too late you're stronger than that; us that talent to get ahead in life

Because yo boy that was watchin yo back; just got shot now he's no longer gifted; but
he died young and black

THE LOOT

Money brings out the worst in you; it makes you high and spending is all you know
how to do

Money make you lose your friends 'cause they know they still owe you your
dividends

Money makes the world go round and round; don't forget money will get you
beat down

At the same time money is making your family act a clown; how soon they forget
that money got their mind play'n tricks

Money comes and money goes only the humble people will have something to show

Money, money, money

GRIND 'N

My man work hard to make ends meet; even though the job he's got
is not really what he seeks

My man is grind'n to get us out these trenches; while he continues to follow
his dreams

I'll stand by my man's side; while encouraging him and lifting his pride

My man is very strong minded indeed; even though he's grinding he keeps me pleased

We've been through thick and thin; I'll never leave my man, 'cause I know he's gonna win

Once the grind'n comes to an end; then he can finally collect all his dividends

CORNER HUSTLE

Bad girl; look'n so pretty why you on the corner hustle? I know you have
to feed yo kids and pay the rent

You keep do'n what you do'n; yo money maker want be worth one red cent

Don't get pulled down the gutter or yo kids will have one dead mother

Get yo self together; you're smarter than a whip; use your mind to make
ends meet and get off the streets

So, hold your head up high and reach for the sky; teach yo kids that the corner
is not where they wanna be, an education is where it's at

FACE OFF

You tried so hard to maintain these two identities; being that hard working
citizen by day and that thug by night

You made sure that your boo had everything; from that big rock on her finger
to that long mink coat that hangs to the floor

You kept the night life away from home 'cause you didn't want any police
knocking on your door

You always held your ground and kept things from getting around town; 'cause
you didn't want your boo worrying about what should she do

Now you're caught between a rock and a hard place; so you decided that you must
come clean and make things right

You have always been a thug; you just quit the game 'cause you realized that all that
money is not the same

Chapter Five

Thoughts of You

SEPTEMBER RAIN

You've been away from me for sometime now; with each day moving by like several dark clouds in the sky

I'm beginning to feel the fall weather rains; while at the same time hiding the hurtful pain that's inside my heart

Another season has come to pass; making me wonder just how our love for each other even last

I think of you day and night; but, my hunger for your love tells me you're alright

Waiting on your return; which I know is near will give me the strength to love you more my dear

There's nothing that can compare to the love we share; because we carry it so deep in our hearts

This makes our love so strong even when we're apart

SEX AS A WEAPON

You make love to me like no other; dam baby I must say you're one bad mother

Using sex as a weapon 'cause its part of your charm while giving me your tongue

You're like 007 using sex as a weapon; but nonetheless you keep sending me to heaven

Never mind what they say; hell you're good at what you do, using sex as a weapon has made women chase after you

It doesn't matter that you got that look; 'cause yo sex got women hooked

Keep using sex as a weapon; because one thing for sure you don't have to worry 'bout me step'n

Long as you keep using sex as a weapon

WINTER BLUES

The days are becoming shorter; while the trees begin to bare their roots

Look into the sky to see why the birds are flying today

It's a cold breeze approaching our way; the nights are clear only because winter is so near

Bundle up before going out the door; 'cause it's not summer any more

Come on in and sit by the fireplace to warm your hands and face

Now fix some homemade soup to eat; then relax 'cause the winter blues can't be beat

MISSING YOU

I'm missing you like crazy; wishing you was here to laugh with me about the
good times we shared

I missed the times; we both got on punishment because we refuse to tell who done it

I missed the times; when people thought we were twins 'cause we had everything alike
right down to our bikes

I missed the times; we read each other thoughts and felt each other's pain even when
we're far apart

I missed the times; we would go club'n and dance the night away 'cause we practiced
our routine earlier that day

I missed the times; when momma took us to church and came out the choir stand to
spank our little hands 'cause we were doing the devils work

I missed the times; when you were always there for me, to include teasing me say'n I
smell that mother's friend 'cause I was pregnant way back then

I missed the times; you would call me and leave me crazy messages, then say well what
are little brothers for?

You kept me going; always making me laugh, so now you left me with only good memories
that we had

I'm missing you

DADDY'S LITTLE GIRL

You've been a great plus in my life

Even though you couldn't watch me grow; well daddy I became someone's beautiful wife

I joined the army to see the world; but nonetheless I'm still daddy's little girl

I made sure I never forgot your face; just remembering how you looked before we left that place

Daddy you always held a spot in my heart; even though we were so far apart

I worried about you a lot; asking GOD to please watch over my pop

Knowing that one day deep in my heart; something will bring us together again

So, until then I want you to remember watching me play; 'cause I was daddy's little girl that day

JUST ME

I write about things that happen to me or thoughts that just run
through me

So, don't judge me for what I see

I write about feelings that set me free

I'm not that caged monkey running up the tree

So, don't patronize me of the emotions that are allowing me
just to be me

DIVA

Just to let you know; I wear designer from head to toe

I have enough bags that got hefty price tags

My shoes are so unique; I need bodyguards so no one can take them off my feet

My clothes have no labels; I draw sketches and get them made at a drop of a dime

'Cause everything must be one of a kind; as you can see I have expensive taste

Being a designer woman is not hard to be; due to the fact that's the DIVA in me

MY LITTLE BROTHER

You always looked up to me; but not knowing that I envied you the most

When we were kids, we did everything together; we made a pledge that we'll
Always stay close

As adults even though we were miles apart you always found a way to reach
My heart

I remember when we were little and momma took me to see you in the hospital
When you were sick

At that moment, I did a silent prayer and asked GOD not to take you away from
Me yet

It's true, on that day GOD made a promise to let you stay; so I guess that time is up

GOD held that promise long enough; yes he took you at a very young age

But, right now you're in heaven center stage

I'll always remember when you walked into a room; you brought smiles upon people's faces

Now my little brother you can do the same in GOD's place rest in peace

DREAMS

Your dreams are what you make them to be; so stop trying to fake it with me

I'm not the one you need to impress; you must have that confidence to know you are better than the rest

Don't you know dreaming is what we all do; without dreams how can we see our desires come true

So, why are you allowing your emotions to pave the way; when your dreams already showed you just what to do

Stop hindering yourself from becoming that person people might see in fortune magazine one day

Dreams are like the rainbow in the sky; keep chasing them 'cause your pot of gold just might be near by

YOU'RE HOLDING BACK

I've given my last, to include the savings I had in the past

I give my part to make ends meet but yet you don't help to
reach that peak

I spend my money on things we need and you still don't take heed

Your pockets are fat just like my kitty cat; but on the same token you
want even buy me a hat

I don't understand why you're still holding back

LOVE

Love brings out uncontrollable emotions

Love is a dangerous game; and can never be played the same

Some people use love in many different ways; watch out for those 'cause they'll keep you on your toes

The word is so strong; it can hurt you down to your soul

They are emotions delt with on a daily basis; 'cause love is truly known to have several faces

It's like the wolf in sheep clothing; when you're not looking it'll steal your heart

Love brings people together; while on the other hand it can pull them apart

Looking back on history the "L" word has remain the same; only the emotions have changed

YOU AND ME

We were criticized from the beginning; you and me

We announced our engagement, they say it wouldn't last; you and me

We had our good times and bad times; you and me but love does conquer all
you and me

On this day we're renewing our vows; you and me because love is better and stronger
a second time around you and me

Our love, trust and faith we have had encourage us to make it last; you and me twenty-five
years from now; we'll look back and say, it always have been just you and me

EMOTIONS

Deep down inside I'm hurt wondering how can this be

We use to be so close you and me nothing could break us apart

We were like Siamese twins just sharing only one heart

You were my best friend; someone I could depend on and be there
until the end

It's so hard to sleep when I know we're fallen apart

We made so much together and encouraged each other to do better

Your priorities were never with me 'cause you're still trying to keep your
old family tree

A decision has to be made; when you finally decide to come around

Pray to GOD that I haven't left town

PLEDGE MY LOVE

I pledge my love for you

My love is so deep it goes through and through making my heart belonging
only to you

My love is so strong when the Lord decide to take you, I must go too 'cause I
can't bear living without you

If your heart goes weak inside; I'll give you mine just to keep you alive

This love I pledge to you comes directly from my heart while hoping nothing
never keep us apart